52 Scottish ! For All Harps

arranged for the harp by
Sylvia Woods

If you play a lever (non-pedal) harp, be sure to set your sharping levers for the key signature before you begin, following any additional instructions written at the beginning of each piece. All other sharping lever changes are written between the treble and bass staves. This chart shows the octaves indicated by the lever changes you'll find in this book. "Middle" (or "Mid") indicates the octave from middle C up to B, and "High" indicates the next higher octave. "Low" indicates the octave below middle C, and "Very Low" is the octave below that.

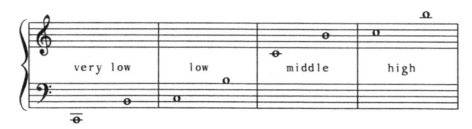

Pedal changes for pedal harps are written below the bass clef staff.

A Note for Pedal Harpists and Advanced Harp Players
Feel free to add more notes to the chords as well as adding arpeggios and glissandos wherever you feel they will be appropriate. And of course, the fingerings indicated may be changed to fit your own preferences.

Companion Cassette
A companion cassette, recorded by Sylvia Woods, is available to go along with this book. Its purpose is to assist harp players learning these beautiful songs. Since many players will want to "play along" with the tape as they are learning, Sylvia has recorded the pieces at a slower speed than they are usually played, and as "straight" as possible, with little expression or rhythmic variation. The tape includes all of the advanced arrangements, but you can play either the easy or the advanced arrangements along with the cassette. Many other books by Sylvia Woods are also available with companion cassettes. For more information, write to the Sylvia Woods Harp Center at the address listed below.

Many thanks to Ellie Choate, Rayven Hockett, Terri Skeoch, and Heidi Spiegel
Cover artwork by Heidi Spiegel

Portrait of Robert Burns by Alexander Nasmyth on page 79
used by permission of the National Portrait Gallery, London, England

All harp arrangements by Sylvia Woods

www.harpcenter.com

© 1997 by Sylvia Woods, Sylvia Woods Harp Center, Woods Music & Books
P.O. Box 223434, Princeville HI 96722 USA

ISBN 0-936661-21-6

Alphabetical Index

Biographical and Historical Notes

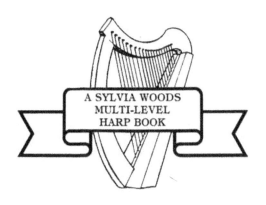

A SYLVIA WOODS
MULTI-LEVEL
HARP BOOK

Annie Laurie
easy harp arrangement

Harp arrangement by Sylvia Woods

Traditional

1. Maxwellton braes are bonnie, where early falls the dew,
And it's there that Annie Laurie gave me her promise true.
Gave me her promise true, which ne'er forgot will be,
And for bonnie Annie Laurie, I'd lay me doon and dee. ➡ ➡

Annie Laurie
advanced harp arrangement

Harp arrangement by Sylvia Woods

Traditional

Slowly

2. Her brow is like the snowdrift, her neck is like the swan,
Her face it is the fairest, that e'er the sun shone on.
That e'er the sun shone on, and dark blue is her e'e,
And for bonnie Annie Laurie, I'd lay me doon and dee.

3. Like dew on the gowan lying, is the fa' o' her fairy feet;
And like winds in summer sighing, her voice is low and sweet.
Her voice is low and sweet, she's a' the world to me,
And for bonnie Annie Laurie, I'd lay me doon and dee.

Auld Lang Syne
easy harp arrangement

Harp arrangement by Sylvia Woods

Words by Robert Burns

Moderately, with expression

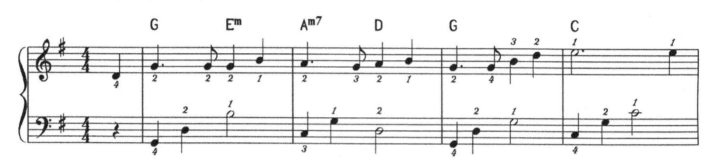

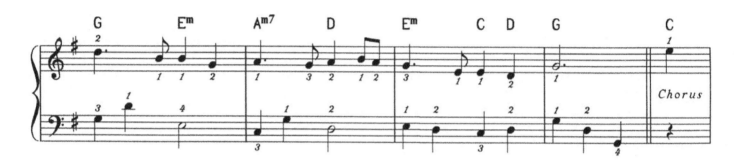

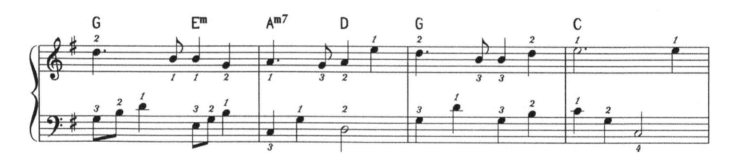

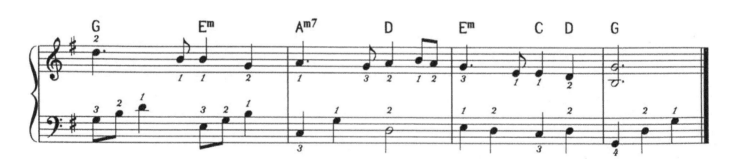

1. Should auld acquaintance be
   forgot,
   And never brought to mind?
   Should auld acquaintance be forgot,
   And days o' lang syne!

CHORUS:
For auld lang syne, my dear
For auld lang syne,
We'll tak a cup o' kindness yet
For auld lang syne!

2. And surely ye'll be your pint-
   stowp,
   And surely I'll be mine,
   And we'll tak a cup o' kindness yet
   For auld lang syne! ➔ ➔

6

Auld Lang Syne
advanced harp arrangement

Harp arrangement by Sylvia Woods

Words by Robert Burns

Moderately, with expression

3. We twa hae run about the braes,
And pou'd the gowans fine,
But we've wander'd mony a weary
  foot
Sin auld lang syne.

4. We twa hae paidl'd in the burn
Frae morning sun till dine,
But seas between us braid hae
  roar'd
Sin auld lang syne.

5. And there's a hand, my trusty
  fiere,
And gie's a hand o' thine,
And we'll tak a right gude willie-
  waught
For auld lang syne!

Ay Waukin, O
easy harp arrangement

Harp arrangement by Sylvia Woods

Words by Robert Burns

Slowly

CHORUS:
Ay waukin, O,
Waukin still and weary;
Sleep I can get nane
For thinking on my dearie.
Ay waukin, O.

1. Simmer's a pleasant time;
Flowers of ev'ry colour,
The water rins o'er the heugh,
And I long for my true lover. ➔ ➔

Ay Waukin, O

advanced harp arrangement

Harp arrangement by Sylvia Woods

Words by Robert Burns

Slowly

2. When I sleep I dream,
When I wauk I'm eerie,
Sleep I can get nane
For thinking on my dearie.

3. Lanely night comes on,
A' the lave are sleepin
I think on my bonnie lad,
And I bleer my een wi' greetin.

Baloo Baleerie
easy harp arrangement

Harp arrangement by Sylvia Woods

Traditional

Slowly

CHORUS:
Baloo, baleerie, baloo, baleerie
Baloo, baleerie, baloo balee.

1. Gang awa' peerie fairies,
Gang awa' peerie fairies,
Gang awa' peerie fairies,
Frae oor ben noo.

2. Doon come the bonny angels,
Doon come the bonny angels,
Doon come the bonny angels,
Tae oor ben noo.

3. Sleep saft my baby,
Sleep saft my baby,
Sleep saft my baby,
In oor ben noo.

Baloo Baleerie
advanced harp arrangement

Harp arrangement by Sylvia Woods

Traditional

Slowly

Scots Language

The words of "Baloo Baleerie" are in Scots, the language of Lowland Scotland. Some linguistic scholars classify Scots as its own language, and not a dialect of English. Most of the words in the glossary on pages 110-111 are Scots. Many are found in the songs of Robert Burns (see page 53) who tended to use "standard English" for his romantic and serious songs, and Scots for his more "earthy" and satirical songs. As you familiarize yourself with the lyrics in this book, the meanings of many of these words will begin to come naturally to you. When in doubt, check the glossary. Remember that many words have multiple meanings, so you'll need to check the context in the songs. By the way, the words "Baloo Baleerie" are nonsense syllables crooned to children in lullabies.

The Birks Of Aberfeldy
easy harp arrangement

Harp arrangement by Sylvia Woods

Words by Robert Burns

CHORUS:
Bonnie lassie, will ye go,
Will ye go, will ye go?
Bonnie lassie, will ye go
To the birks of Aberfeldy?

1. Now simmer blinks on flow'ry
braes,
And o'er the crystal streamlets plays;
Come, let us spend the lightsome days
In the birks of Aberfeldy.

2. The little birdies blythely sing,
While o'er their heads the hazels hing,
Or lightly flit on wanton wing
In the birks of Aberfeldy. ➙ ➙

12

The Birks Of Aberfeldy
advanced harp arrangement

Harp arrangement by Sylvia Woods

Words by Robert Burns

Merrily

3. The braes ascend like lofty wa's,
The foaming stream, deep-roaring fa's
O'erhung wi' fragrant-spreading shaws
The birks of Aberfeldy.

4. The hoary cliffs are crown'd wi flowers,
White o'er the linns the burnie pours,
And, rising, weets wi' misty showers
The birks of Aberfeldy. *(Lyrics cont. on pg. 108)*

The Blue Bells Of Scotland

easy harp arrangement

Harp arrangement by Sylvia Woods

Words by Mrs. Jordan

Moderately

1. Oh where, tell me where is your Highland laddie gone?
Oh where, tell me where is your Highland laddie gone?
He's gone wi' steaming banners where noble deeds are done,
And it's oh, in my heart I wish him safe at home.

2. Oh where, tell me where did your Highland laddie dwell?
Oh where, tell me where did your Highland laddie dwell?
He dwelt in bonnie Scotland, where blooms the sweet blue bell,
And it's oh, in my heart I lo'e my laddie well. ➤ ➤

The Blue Bells Of Scotland
advanced harp arrangement

Harp arrangement by Sylvia Woods

Words by Mrs. Jordan

Moderately

3. Oh what, tell me what does your Highland laddie wear?
Oh what, tell me what does your Highland laddie wear?
A bonnet with a lofty plume, and on his breast a plaid,
And it's oh, in my heart I lo'e my Highland lad.

4. Oh what, tell me what if your Highland lad be slain?
Oh what, tell me what if your Highland lad be slain?
Oh, no, true love will be his guard and bring him safe again.
For it's oh, my heart would break if my Highland lad were slain!

The Boatie Rows
easy harp arrangement

Harp arrangement by Sylvia Woods

Words by John Ewen

Happily

1. O weel may the boatie row,
And better may she speed,
O weel may the boatie row
That wins the bairns' bread.
The boatie rows, the boatie rows,
The boatie rows indeed,
And happy be the lot of a'
That wishes her to speed.

2. I cast my lines in Largo Bay,
And fishes I got nine;
There's three to boil and three to fry
And three to bait the line.
The boatie rows, the boatie rows,
The boatie rows fu' weel;
And muckle lighter is the lade,
When love bears up the creel.

3. O weel may the boatie row,
That fills a heavy creel,
And clead us a' frae head to feet
And buys our parritch meal.
The boatie rows, the boatie rows,
The boatie rows indeed;
And happy be the lot of a'
That wish the boatie speed.

4. When Sawnie, Jock and Janetie
Are up and gotten lear
They'll help to gar the boatie row,
And lighten a' our care.
The boatie rows, the boatie rows,
The boatie rows fu' weel;
And lightsome be her heart that bears
The murlain and the creel! ➙ ➙

16

The Boatie Rows
advanced harp arrangement

Harp arrangement by Sylvia Woods

Words by John Ewen

Happily

5. And when wi' age we're worn down,
And hirplin round the door;
They'll row to keep us hale and warm,
As we did them before.

The boatie rows, the boatie rows,
The boatie rows fu' weel;
And muckle lighter is the lade,
When love bears up the creel.

Bonnie Bell
(The Smiling Spring)
easy harp arrangement

Harp arrangement by Sylvia Woods

Words by Robert Burns

Sweetly and happily

1. The smiling Spring comes in rejoicing,
And surly Winter grimly flies;
Now crystal clear are the falling waters,
And bonny blue are the sunny skies.
Fresh o'er the mountains breaks forth the morning,
The ev'ning gilds the ocean's swell;
All creatures joy in the sun's returning,
And I rejoice in my bonnie Bell.   ➔ ➔

18

Bonnie Bell
(The Smiling Spring)
advanced harp arrangement

Harp arrangement by Sylvia Woods

Words by Robert Burns

Sweetly and happily

2. The flow'ry Spring leads sunny summer,
And yellow Autumn presses near,
Then in his turn comes gloomy winter,
Till smiling Spring again appear.
Thus seasons dancing, life advancing,
Old Time and Nature their changes tell;
But never ranging, still unchanging,
I adore my bonnie Bell.

Bonnie Dundee
easy harp arrangement

Harp arrangement by Sylvia Woods

Traditional

1. To the Lords of Convention 'twas Claverhouse spoke,
Ere the King's crown go down there are crowns to be broke;
So each cavalier who loves honour and me,
Let him follow the bonnets o' Bonnie Dundee.

Chorus:
Come fill up my cup, come fill up my can,

Come saddle my horses, and call out my men;
Unhook the West Port and let us gae free,
For it's up with the bonnets o' Bonnie Dundee!

2. Dundee he is mounted, he rides up the street,
The bells they ring backward, the drums they are beat;
But the provost (douce man) said: "Just e'en let it be,
For the town is weel rid o' that deil o' Dundee."
(Lyrics continued on page 108)

Bonnie Dundee
advanced harp arrangement

Harp arrangement by Sylvia Woods

Traditional

Like a March

Bonnie Wee Thing
easy harp arrangement

Harp arrangement by Sylvia Woods

Words by Robert Burns

Lyrics are on page 108

Bonnie Wee Thing
advanced harp arrangement

Harp arrangement by Sylvia Woods

Words by Robert Burns

Braw, Braw Lads

Harp arrangement by Sylvia Woods
Moderately

Words by Robert Burns

easy

1. Braw, braw lads on Yarrow braes,
They rove amang the blooming heather;
But Yarrow braes nor Ettrick shaws,
Can match the lads o' Galla Water.

2. But there is ane, a secret ane,
Aboon them a' I lo'e him better;
And I'll be his, and he'll be mine,
The bonnie lad o' Galla Water.

3. Altho' his daddie was nae laird,
And tho' I hae nae meikle tocher;
Yet, rich in kindest, truest love,
We'll tent our flocks by Galla Water.

4. It ne'er was wealth, it ne'er was wealth,
That coft contentment, peace or pleasure;
The bands and bliss o' mutual love,
O, that's the chiefest warld's treasure!

advanced

Buy Broom Besoms

Harp arrangement by Sylvia Woods
Moderately and continuously

Collected by Robert Burns

easy

1. I maun hae a wife, whatsoe'er she be,
An' she be a woman, that's enough for me.

CHORUS:
Buy broom besoms! Wha will buy them noo?
Fine heather ringers, better never grew.

2. If that she be bonny, I shall think her right,
If that she be ugly, where's the odds at night?

3. O, an' she be young, how happy shall I be
If that she be auld, the sooner she will dee.

4. If that she be fruitfu', O what joy is there!
If she should be barren, less will be my care.

5. If she like a drappie, she and I'll agree,
If she dinna like it, there's the mair for me.

6. Be she green or grey, be she black or fair,
Let her be a woman, I shall seek nae mair.

advanced

Ca' The Yowes To The Knowes
easy harp arrangement

Harp arrangement by Sylvia Woods

Words by Robert Burns

Tranquilly

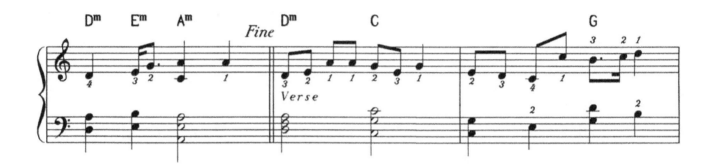

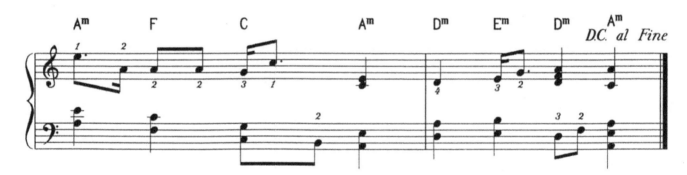

CHORUS:
Ca' the yowes to the knowes.
Ca' them where the heather grows,
Ca' them where the burnie rowes,
My bonnie dearie.

1. Hark, the mavis' e'ening sang
Sounding Clouden's woods amang,
Then a-faulding let us gang,
My bonnie dearie.

2. We'll gae down by Clouden side,
Thro' the hazels, spreading wide
O'er the waves that sweetly glide
To the moon sae clearly. ➔ ➔

Ca' The Yowes To The Knowes

advanced harp arrangement

Harp arrangement by Sylvia Woods

Words by Robert Burns

Tranquilly

3. Yonder Clouden's silent towers
Where, at moonshine's midnight hours,
O'er the dewy bending flowers
Fairies dance sae cheery.

4. Ghaist nor bogle shalt thou fear,
Thou'rt to Love and Heav'n sae dear,
Nocht of ill may come thee near,
My bonnie dearie.

5. Fair and lovely as thou art,
Thou hast stown my very heart;
I can die -- but canna part,
My bonnie dearie.

Charlie Is My Darling

easy harp arrangement

Harp arrangement by Sylvia Woods

Words by Lady Nairne

Lever harp players: set the high D# before you begin.

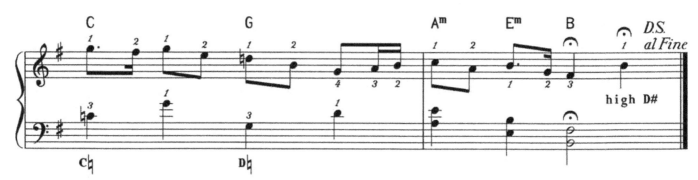

CHORUS:
Oh, Charlie is my darling,
My darling, my darling!
Charlie is my darling,
The young Chevalier.

1. 'Twas on a Monday morning,
Right early in the year,
When Charlie came to our town,
The young Chevalier.

2. As he cam' marchin' up the street,
The pipes played loud and clear,
And a' the folks cam' rinnin' out,
To meet the Chevalier.

3. Wi' Highland bonnets on their heads,
And claymores bright and clear,
They cam' to fight for Scotland's right,
And the young Chevalier.

4. They've left their bonnie Hieland hills,
Their wives and bairnies dear,
To draw the sword for Scotland's lord,
The young Chevalier.

5. Oh, there were mony beating hearts,
And mony a hope and fear,
And mony were the pray'rs put up
For the young Chevalier.

Charlie Is My Darling
advanced harp arrangement

Harp arrangement by Sylvia Woods

Words by Lady Nairne

Lever harp players: set the high D# before you begin.

Lightly

Bonnie Prince Charlie

It has been said that more songs have been written about Bonnie Prince Charlie than any other man in history. Also known as "the Young Pretender" and "the Chevalier", Charles Edward Stuart (1720-1788) was a dashing and controversial youth who staked everything on his bid to restore the Stuarts to the throne of England and Scotland. With his Jacobite supporters, he won several battles in 1745, but was finally soundly defeated by the English at Culloden in April 1746. For the next five months he was a fugitive with a price of £30,000 on his head, the equivalent of about a half a million pounds in today's money. Many loyal men and women of the clans risked their lives to hide or protect him. The most famous of these was Flora MacDonald. With the fugitive prince disguised as her maid, she took him "over the sea to Skye", as commemorated in the "Skye Boat Song" (see pages 98-99). A few months later he sailed for France, and remained there until his death in 1788.

Comin' Thro' The Rye

easy harp arrangement

Harp arrangement by Sylvia Woods

Words by Robert Burns

1. Gin' a body meet a body
Comin' thro' the rye;
Gin' a body kiss a body
Need a body cry?
Ilka lassie has her laddie
Nane they say ha'e I;
Yet a' the lads they smile at me
When comin' thro' the rye.

2. Gin' a body meet a body
Comin' frae the well;
Gin' a body kiss a body
Need a body tell?
Ilka lassie has her laddie
Ne'er a ane ha'e I
But a' the lads they smile on me
When comin' thro' the rye. ➔ ➔

Comin' Thro' The Rye
advanced harp arrangement

Harp arrangement by Sylvia Woods

Words by Robert Burns

3. Gin' a body meet a body
Comin' frae the town;
Gin' a body greet a body
Need a body frown?
Ilka lassie has her laddie
Nane they say ha'e I;
But a' the lads they lo'e me weel,
And what the waur am I.

4. Amang the train there is a swain
I dearly lo'e mysel';
But whaur his hame, or what his name,
I dinna care to tell.
Ilka lassie has her laddie,
Nane they say ha'e I;
But a' the lads they lo'e me weel,
And what the waur am I.

Corn Rigs Are Bonnie
easy harp arrangement

Harp arrangement by Sylvia Woods

Words by Robert Burns

Happily

Lyrics are on page 108

Corn Rigs Are Bonnie
advanced harp arrangement

Harp arrangement by Sylvia Woods

Words by Robert Burns

Happily

Dumbarton's Drums
easy harp arrangement

Harp arrangement by Sylvia Woods

Traditional

Tenderly

1. Dumbarton's drums they sound so bonnie,
And they remind me o' my Johnnie,
Such fond delight doth steal upon me
When Johnny kneels and kisses me.

2. Across the fields o' boundin' heather
Dumbarton tolls the hour of pleasure
A song of love that's without measure
When Johnnie sings his sangs tae me.

3. 'Tis he alone that can delight me
His rovin' eye, it doth invite me,
And when his tender arms enfold me
The blackest night doth turn and flee.

4. My Johnnie is a handsome laddie
And though he is Dumbarton's caddie,
Some day I'll be a captain's lady
When Johnnie tends his vows tae me.

Dumbarton's Drums
advanced harp arrangement

Harp arrangement by Sylvia Woods

Traditional

Tenderly

Earl of Dumbarton

The drums mentioned in this song are those of a British regiment under the command of the Earl of Dumbarton. He was commander of the Royal forces in Scotland during the reign of Charles II and James II. The Earl suppressed the rebellion of Argyle in 1685.

Duncan Gray
easy harp arrangement

Harp arrangement by Sylvia Woods

Words by Robert Burns

Lively, but not too fast

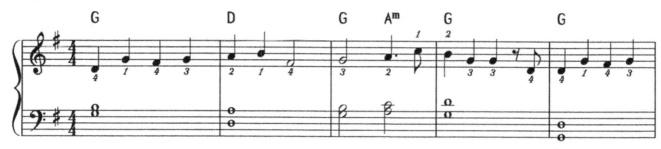

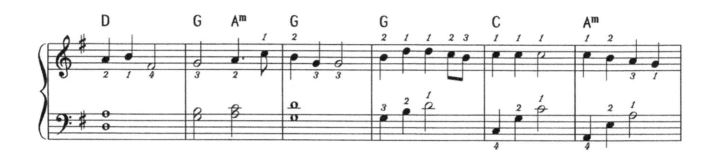

1. Duncan Gray cam' here to woo,
Ha, ha, the wooing o't,
On blythe Yule night, when we were fu',
Ha, ha, the wooing o't.
Maggie coost her head fu' heigh,
Look'd asklent and unco skeigh.
Gart poor Duncan stand abeigh;
Ha, ha, the wooing o't.

2. Duncan fleech'd and Duncan pray'd;
Ha, ha, the wooing o't,
Meg was deaf as Ailsa Craig,
Ha, ha, the wooing o't,

Duncan sigh'd baith out and in,
Grat his een baith blear'd and blin',
Spak o' lowpin o'er a linn;
Ha, ha, the wooing o't.

3. Time and Chance are but a tide,
Ha, ha, the wooing o't,
Slighted love is sair to bide,
Ha, ha, the wooing o't,
"Shall I like a fool," quoth he,
"For a haughty hizzie die?
She may gae to -- France for me!"
Ha, ha, the wooing o't. ➙ ➙

Duncan Gray
advanced harp arrangement

Harp arrangement by Sylvia Woods

Words by Robert Burns

Lively, but not too fast

4. How it comes let doctors tell,
Ha, ha, the wooing o't,
Meg grew sick, as he grew hale,
Ha, ha, the wooing o't.
Something in her bosom wrings,
For relief a sigh she brings;
And O! her een they spak sic things!
Ha, ha, the wooing o't.

5. Duncan was a lad o' grace,
Ha, ha, the wooing o't,
Maggie's was a piteous case,
Ha, ha, the wooing o't;
Duncan could na be her death,
Swelling Pity smoor'd his wrath;
Now they're crouse and canty baith,
Ha, ha, the wooing o't.

Flow Gently Sweet Afton
easy harp arrangement

Harp arrangement by Sylvia Woods

Words by Robert Burns

There are several melodies that are used with these words. This melody is the best known in Scotland.

Lever harp players: the high F and the low F should be set as F naturals before you begin. They will not change throughout the piece.

Peacefully

1. Flow gently, sweet Afton, among thy green braes,
Flow gently, I'll sing thee a song in thy praise;
My Mary's asleep by thy murmuring stream,
Flow gently, sweet Afton, disturb not her dream!

2. Thou stock dove whose echo resounds thro' the glen,
Ye wild whistling blackbirds in yon thorny den,
Thou green-crested lapwing, thy screaming forbear,
I charge you, disturb not my slumbering fair!

3. How lofty, sweet Afton, thy neighbouring hills,
Far mark'd with the courses of clear, winding rills;
There daily I wander, as noon rises high,
My flocks and my Mary's sweet cot in my eye.

4. How pleasant thy banks and green valleys below,
Where wild in the woodlands the primroses blow;
There oft, as mild ev'ning weeps over the lea,
The sweet-scented birk shades my Mary and me.

➨ ➨

Flow Gently Sweet Afton
advanced harp arrangement

Harp arrangement by Sylvia Woods

Words by Robert Burns

Lever harp players: the high F and the low F should be set as F naturals before you begin. They will not change throughout the piece.

5. The crystal stream, Afton, how lovely it glides,
And winds by the cot where my Mary resides;
How wanton thy waters her snowy feet lave,
As, gathering sweet flow'rets, she stems thy clear wave.

6. Flow gently, sweet Afton, among thy green braes,
Flow gently, I'll sing thee a song in thy praise;
My Mary's asleep by thy murmuring stream,
Flow gently, sweet Afton, disturb not her dream!

The Flowers O' The Forest

easy harp arrangement

Harp arrangement by Sylvia Woods

Traditional

There are two different melodies associated with this song. This melody was originally an old harp tune, and is often played at funerals.

Lever harp players: the middle F should be set as F natural before you begin. It will not change throughout the piece.

Slowly

1. I've heard them liltin' at our ewe milkin'
Lasses a-liltin' before the dawn of day;
But now they are moanin' on ilka green loanin'
The Flowers o' the Forest are a' wede away.

2. At bughts in the mornin, nae blythe lads are scorning,
The lasses are lonely, and dowie, and wae;
Nae daffin', nae gabbin', but sighing and sabbing,
Ilk ane lifts her leglin and hies away.

3. In hairst, at the shearing, nae youths now are jeering,
The bandsters are lyart, and runkled and grey;
At fair, or at preaching, nae wooing, nae fleeching,
The Flowers o' the Forest are a' wede away.

4. At e'en, in the gloaming nae swankies are roaming,
'Bout stacks wi' the lasses at bogle to play;
But ilk maid sits drearie, lamenting her dearie,
The Flowers o' the Forest are a' wede away.

5. Dool and wae to the order, sent our lads to the border!
The English, for aince, by guile wan the day;
The Flowers o' the Forest, that fought aye the foremost,
The pride o' our land, lie cauld in the clay.

6. We hear nae mair lilting at our ewe-milking,
Women an' bairns are heartless an' wae;
Sighin' an' moanin' on ilka green loanin' -
The Flowers o' the Forest are a' wede away.

The Flowers O' The Forest
advanced harp arrangement

Harp arrangement by Sylvia Woods

Traditional

Lever harp players: the middle F should be set as F natural before you begin. It will not change throughout the piece.

Slowly

Battle of Flodden

The words of this song speak of the Battle of Flodden on September 9, 1513 when King James IV and much of the Scottish nobility were slain by the troops of Henry VIII. The King, 9 earls, 14 lords, the chiefs of many Highland clans, and thousands of soldiers were massacred.

King James IV's granddaughter was Mary, Queen of Scots, who became ruler of Scotland in 1542.

Green Grow The Rashes, O!
easy harp arrangement

Harp arrangement by Sylvia Woods

Words by Robert Burns

Lever harp players: when you sharp the G at the end of the 2nd line, keep your left hand up by the lever, ready for the natural.

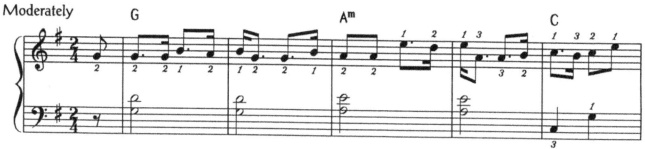

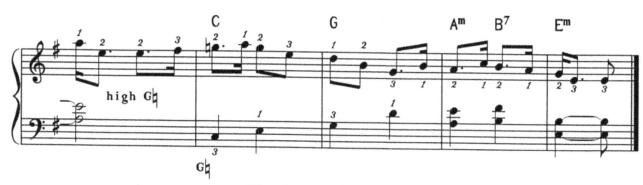

1. There's nought but care on ev'ry han',
In ev'ry hour that passes, O,
What signifies the life o' man,
An 'twere na for the lasses, O?

CHORUS:
Green grow the rashes, O,
Green grow the rashes, O;
The sweetest hours that e'er I spent,
Are spent amang the lasses, O!

2. The warldly race may riches chase,
An' riches still may fly them, O;
An' tho' at last they catch them fast,
Their hearts can ne'er enjoy them, O. ➔ ➔

42

Green Grow The Rashes, O!
advanced harp arrangement

Harp arrangement by Sylvia Woods

Words by Robert Burns

Moderately

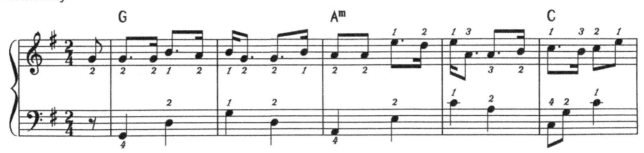

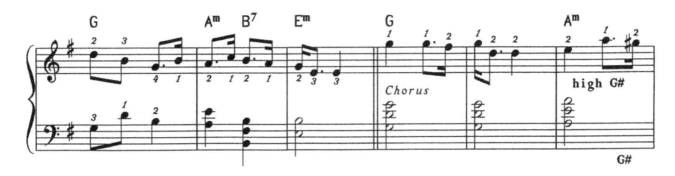

3. But gie me a canty hour at e'en,
My arms about my dearie, O;
An' warldly cares, an' warldly men,
May a' gae tapsalteerie, O!

4. For you sae douce, wha sneer at this;
Ye're nought but senseless asses, O:
The wisest man the warld e'er saw,
He dearly lo'ed the lasses, O.

5. Auld Nature swears, the lovely dears
Her noblest work she classes, O:
Her prentice han' she tried on man,
An' then she made the lasses, O.

Hame, Hame, Hame
easy harp arrangement

Harp arrangement by Sylvia Woods

Traditional

Slowly

1. Hame, hame, hame, O hame fain wad I be,
Hame, hame, hame to my ain countrie!
There's an eye that ever weeps, and a fair face will be fain,
As I pass thro' Annanwater wi' my bonnie bands again;
When the flow'r is in the bud and the leaf upon the tree,
The lark shall sing me hame to my ain countrie.

2. Hame, hame, hame, O hame fain wad I be,
Hame, hame, hame to my ain countrie!
The green leaf o' loyaltie is beginning for to fa',
And the bonnie white rose it is withering and a';
But I'll water't wi' the bluid o' usurping tyrannie,
And green it will grow in my ain countrie.

➔ ➔

44

Hame, Hame, Hame

advanced harp arrangement

Harp arrangement by Sylvia Woods

Traditional

Slowly

3. Hame, hame, hame, O hame fain wad I be,
Hame, hame, hame to my ain countrie!
The great now are gane, a' who ventur'd for to save,

And the new grass is growing above their bluidy grave,
But the sun in the mirk blinks blythe in my e'e,
I'll shine on ye yet in yer ain countrie.

Hieland Laddie

easy harp arrangement

Harp arrangement by Sylvia Woods

Traditional

Lively

1. Will ye go to Inverness, Bonnie laddie, Hieland laddie?
There you'll see the Hieland dress, Bonnie laddie, Hieland laddie.
Philabeg and bonnet blue, Bonnie laddie, Hieland laddie,
For the lad that wears the trews, Bonnie laddie, Hieland laddie.

2. Geordie sits in Charlie's chair, Bonnie laddie, Hieland laddie,
Had I my will he'd no sit there, Bonnie laddie, Hieland laddie.
Ne'er reflect on sorrows past, Bonnie laddie, Hieland laddie,
Charlie will be King at last, Bonnie laddie, Hieland laddie.

3. Time and tide come round to a', Bonnie laddie, Hieland laddie,
And upstart pride will get a fa', Bonnie laddie, Hieland laddie,
Keep up your heart, for Charlie fight, Bonnie laddie, Hieland laddie,
Come what may, ye've done what's right, Bonnie laddie, Hieland laddie.

Hieland Laddie
advanced harp arrangement

Harp arrangement by Sylvia Woods

Traditional

Lively

Alternate Lyrics

1. Where ha'e ye been a' the day, Bonnie laddie, Hieland laddie?
Saw ye him that's far away, Bonnie laddie, Hieland laddie?
On his head a bonnet blue, Bonnie laddie, Hieland laddie,
Tartan plaid and Highland trew, Bonnie laddie, Hieland laddie!

2. When he drew his gude braid sword, Bonnie laddie, Hieland laddie,
Then he gave his royal word, Bonnie laddie, Hieland laddie,
That frae the field he ne'er would flee, Bonnie laddie, Hieland laddie,
But wi' his friends would live or dee, Bonnie laddie, Hieland laddie.

Ho Ro My Nut-Brown Maiden

easy harp arrangement

Harp arrangement by Sylvia Woods

Translated from the Gaelic by John Stuart Blackie

Lively

Chorus:
Ho-ro, my nut-brown maiden,
Hi-ri, my nut-brown maiden,
Ho-ro, ro maiden.
For she's the maid for me.

1. Her eye so mildly beaming,
Her look so frank and free,
In waking and in dreaming,
Is ever more with me.

2. O Mary, mild-eyed Mary,
By land or on the sea.
Though time and tide may vary,
My heart beats true to thee.

3. In Glasgow or Dunedin
Were maidens fair to see,
But never a Lowland maiden
Could lure mine eyes from thee. ➡ ➡

48

Ho Ro My Nut-Brown Maiden

advanced harp arrangement

Harp arrangement by Sylvia Woods
Lively

Translated from the Gaelic by John Stuart Blackie

4. With thy fair face before me,
How sweetly flew the hour,
When all thy beauty o'er me
Came streaming in its power.

5. The face with kindness glowing,
The face that hides no guile,
The light grace of thy going,
The witchcraft of thy smile!

6. And since from thee I parted,
A long and weary while,

I wander heavy hearted
With longing for thy smile.

7. Mine eyes that never vary
From pointing to the glen,
Where blooms my Highland Mary
Like wild rose 'neath the ben.

8. And when with blossoms laden
Bright summer comes again,
I'll fetch my nut-brown maiden
Down from the bonny glen.

I Aince Lo'ed a Lass
easy harp arrangement

Harp arrangement by Sylvia Woods

Traditional

Lever harp players: the middle F and the very low F should be set as F naturals before you begin. They will not change throughout the piece.

Moderately

1. I aince lo'ed a lass, an I lo'ed her sae weel,
I hated a' ithers that spoke o' her ill.
But noo she's rewarded me weel for my love,
For she's gone to be wed tae anither.

2. When I saw my love tae the kirk go
Wi' bride and bride maidens she made a fine show
And I followed on wi' a hairt fu' o' woe
For she's gone tae be wed tae anither.

3. When I saw my love sit doon tae dine
I sat doon beside her and poured oot the wine
And I drank tae the lassie that should hae been mine,
But she's gone tae be wed tae anither. → →

I Aince Lo'ed a Lass

advanced harp arrangement

Harp arrangement by Sylvia Woods

Traditional

Lever harp players: the middle F and the very low F should be set as F naturals before you begin. They will not change throughout the piece.

Moderately

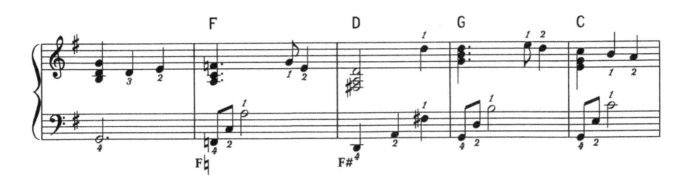

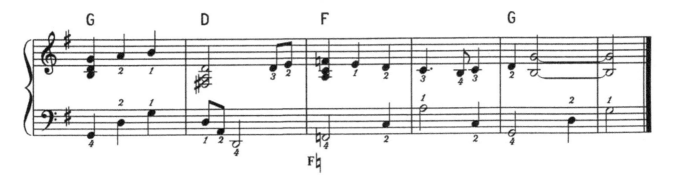

4. The men o' yon forest they askit o' me
"How many strawberries grow in the saut sea?"
I answered them back wi' a tear in my e'e
"How many ships sail in the forest?"

5. O dig me a grave and dig it sae deep
And cover it owre wi' flooers sae sweet
And I will lie doon there and tak' a lang sleep,
And maybe in time I'll forget her.

I'll Ay Ca' In By Yon Toun

easy harp arrangement

Harp arrangement by Sylvia Woods

Words by Robert Burns

Brightly and happily, with animation

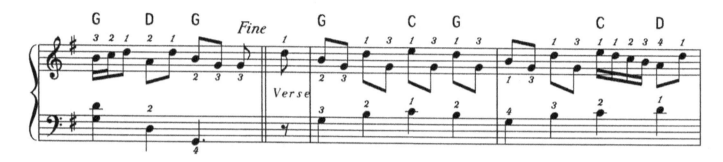

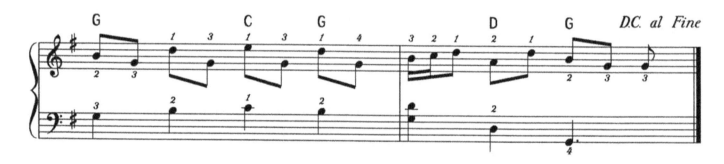

CHORUS:

I'll ay ca' in by yon toun
And by yon garden green again,
I'll ay ca' in by yon toun
And see my bonny Jean again.

1. There's nane shall ken and nane can guess
What brings me back the gate again,
But she, my fairest faithfu' lass,
And stowlins we shall meet again.

2. She'll wander by the aiken tree
When trysting time draws near again;
And when her lovely form I see,
O haith! she's doubly dear again.

I'll Ay Ca' In By Yon Toun

advanced harp arrangement

Harp arrangement by Sylvia Woods

Words by Robert Burns

Brightly and happily, with animation

Robert Burns

More than half of the songs in this book were written or collected by Robert Burns (1759 - 1796), the most famous of Scottish poets and lyricists. He was born at Alloway, Ayrshire on January 25, 1759, the son of a tenant farmer, and spent his youth in poverty. Although he only had a few years of schooling, he was an avid reader. His first book of poetry was published in 1786, and he became a success in fashionable society in Edinburgh. In 1787 he met James Johnson who had just prepared the first volume of *The Scots Musical Museum*, in which he proposed to collect all the traditional Scottish songs with printable words. Because of Burns' enthusiasm for the project, he became the editor of the next 5 volumes. It was for these collections and also George Thomson's *Select Collection of Original Scotish Airs* that Burns began writing more than 300 lyrics, all composed to specific airs. He collected words and music, sometimes only fragments, and added lyrics or stanzas of his own where words were either lacking, or indecent. He wrote both in standard English and in the Scots dialect. (See page 11.)

Jock O'Hazeldean

easy harp arrangement

Harp arrangement by Sylvia Woods

Words by Sir Walter Scott

1. "Why weep ye by the tide, lady?
Why weep ye be the tide?
I'll wed ye to my youngest son,
And ye shall be his bride.
And ye shall be his bride, lady,
Sae comely to be seen."
But aye she loot the tears down fa';
For Jock o' Hazeldean.

2. "Now let this willfu' grief be done,
And dry that cheek so pale,
Young Frank is chief of Errington,
And lord o' Langley dale.
His step is first in peaceful ha',
His sword in battle keen."
But aye she loot the tears down fa';
For Jock o' Hazeldean. → →

Jock O'Hazeldean
advanced harp arrangement

Harp arrangement by Sylvia Woods

Words by Sir Walter Scott

3. "A chain o' gold ye shall not lack,
Nor braid to bind your hair;
Nor mettled hound, nor managed hawk,
Nor palfrey fresh and fair.
And you the foremost of them a'
Shall ride, our forest queen -- "
But aye she loot the tears down fa';
For Jock o' Hazeldean.

4. The kirk was decked at morning tide,
The tapers glimmered fair,
The priest and bridegroom wait the bride,
And dame and knight were there.
They sought her baith by bower and ha',
The lady was not seen;
She's o'er the border and awa'
Wi' Jock o' Hazeldean.

John Anderson, My Jo
easy harp arrangement

Harp arrangement by Sylvia Woods

Words by Robert Burns

Lever harp players: Set the middle F sharp before you begin.

Slowly

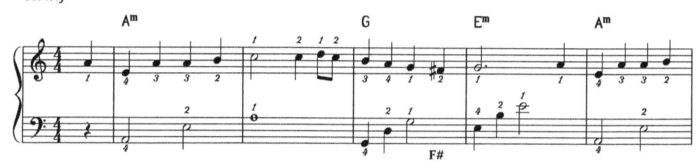

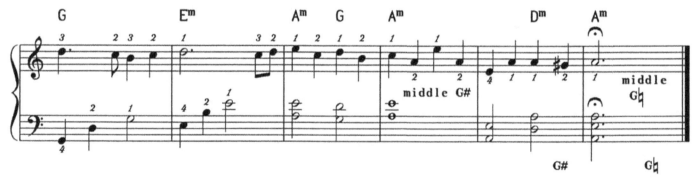

1. John Anderson, my jo, John, when we were first acquent,
Your locks were like the raven, your bonnie brow was brent;
But now your brow is bald, John, your locks are like the snaw,
But blessings on your frosty pow, John Anderson, my jo.

2. John Anderson, my jo, John, I wonder what you mean,
To rise so soon in the morning, an' sit up so late at e'en;
Ye'll blear out a' your een, John; and why should you do so?
Gang sooner to your bed at e'en, John Anderson, my jo.

3. John Anderson, my jo, John, when nature first began
To try her canny hand, John, her master work was Man;
And you among them a', John, sae trig from top to toe,
She proved to be nae journey-wark. John Anderson, my jo. → →

John Anderson, My Jo
advanced harp arrangement

Harp arrangement by Sylvia Woods   Words by Robert Burns

Lever harp players: Set the middle F sharp before you begin.

Slowly

4. John Anderson, my jo, John, you were my first conceit,
An' ye need na think it strange, John, thou' I ca' ye trim and neat:
Tho' some folks say ye're auld, John, I never think ye so,
But I think ye're ay the same to me, John Anderson, my jo.

5. John Anderson, my jo, John, we've seen our bairn's bairns.
And yet, my dear John Anderson, I'm happy in your arms;
And sae are ye in mine, John -- I'm sure ye'll ne'er say no,
Tho' the days are gane that we hae seen, John Anderson, my jo.

6. John Anderson, my jo, John, what pleasure does it gie,
To hae sae mony sproots, John, spring up 'tween you an' me?
An' ilka lad an' lass, John, in our footsteps to go,
Maks heaven here on earth, John Anderson, my jo.   *(Lyrics continued on pg 108)*

The Keel Row
easy harp arrangement

Harp arrangement by Sylvia Woods

Traditional

Brightly

1. Oh, who is like my Johnnie,
Sae leish, sae blythe, sae bonnie!
He's foremost 'mang the mony
Keel lads o' coaly Tyne.
He'll set or row sae tightly,
Or in the dance sae sprightly,
He'll cut and shuffle slightly,
'Tis true, were he not mine.

CHORUS:
Weel may the keel row,
The keel row, the keel row.
Weel may the keel row,
That my lad's in.

2. He has no mair o' learning,
Than tells his weekly earning;

Yet right frae wrang discerning,
Though brave, nae bruiser he.
Though he no worth a plack is,
His ain coat on his back is,
And nane can say that black is
The white o' Johnnie's e'e.

(Lyrics continued on page 108)

The Keel Row
advanced harp arrangement

Harp arrangement by Sylvia Woods

Traditional

Brightly

Kelvin Grove
easy harp arrangement

Harp arrangement by Sylvia Woods

Words by Thomas Lyle

Sweetly

1. Let us haste to Kelvin Grove, bonnie lassie, O!
Thro' its mazes let us rove, bonnie lassie, O!
Where the rose in all her pride paints the hollow dingle side,
Where the midnight fairies glide, bonnie lassie, O!

2. Let us wander by the mill, bonnie lassie, O!
To the cove beside the rill bonnie lassie, O!
Where the glens rebound the call of the roaring waterfall,
Thro' the mountains rocky hall, bonnie lassie, O!

3. O Kelvin banks are fair, bonnie lassie, O!
When in summer we are there, bonnie lassie, O!
There the Maypink's crimson plume throws a soft but sweet perfume
Round the yellow banks of broom, bonnie lassie, O!

4. Though I dare not call thee mine, bonnie lassie, O!
As the smile of fortune's thine, bonnie lassie, O!
Yet with fortune on my side, I could stay thy father's pride,
And win thee for my bride, bonnie lassie, O! → →

Kelvin Grove
advanced harp arrangement

Harp arrangement by Sylvia Woods

Words by Thomas Lyle

5. But the frowns o' fortune lower, bonnie lassie, O!
On thy lover, at this hour, bonnie lassie, O!
Ere yon golden orb of day wake the warblers on the spray,
From this land I must away, bonnie lassie, O!

6. Then farewell to Kelvin Grove, bonnie lassie, O!
And adieu to all I love, bonnie lassie, O!
To the river winding clear, to the fragrant scented brier,
E'en to thee, of all most dear, bonnie lassie, O!

7. When upon a foreign shore, bonnie lassie, O!
Should I fall 'midst battle's roar, bonnie lassie, O!
Then, Helen, should'st thou hear of thy lover on his bier,
To his mem'ry shed a tear, bonnie lassie, O!

Land O' The Leal

easy harp arrangement

Harp arrangement by Sylvia Woods
This is the same basic tune as "Scots Wha Hae", but at a much slower tempo.

Words by Lady Nairne

Slowly, stately, and expressively

1. I'm wearin' awa', Jean, like snaw-wreaths in thaw, Jean,
I'm wearin' awa' tae the Land o' the Leal.
There's nae sorrow there, Jean, there's neither cauld nor care, Jean,
The day is aye fair in the Land o' the Leal.

2. Ye aye were leal and true, Jean, your task is ended noo, Jean,
And I'll welcome you tae the Land o' the Leal.
Our bonnie bairn's there, Jean, she was baith guid and fair, Jean,
And oh, we grudged her sair tae the Land o' the Leal.

3. So dry that tearfu' e'e, Jean, my soul langs tae be free, Jean,
And angels wait on me tae the Land o' the Leal.
So fare thee weel my ain Jean, this world's care is vain, Jean,
We'll meet and aye be fain, tae the Land o' the Leal.

Land O' The Leal
advanced harp arrangement

Harp arrangement by Sylvia Woods

Words by Lady Nairne

Slowly, stately, and expressively

Lady Nairne

Lady Caroline Nairne (1766 - 1845) wrote the lyrics to many popular
Scottish songs. In this book, her lyrics are found in "Charlie Is My
Darling", "Land O' The Leal", "The Rowan Tree", and "Will Ye No
Come Back Again". During her lifetime some of her songs were printed
in The Scottish Minstrel under her pen-name "Mrs Bogan of Bogan".
Others appeared in 1846 in Lays from Strathearn.

Lassie Wi' The Lint-White Locks
easy harp arrangement

Harp arrangement by Sylvia Woods

Words by Robert Burns

Moderately

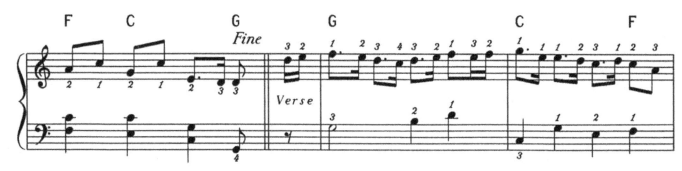

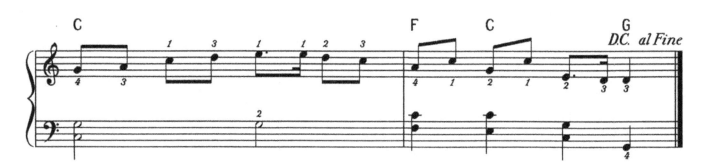

CHORUS:
Lassie wi' the lint-white locks
Bonnie lassie, artless lassie
Wilt thou wi' me tent the flocks --
Wilt thou be my dearie, O?

1. Now Nature cleeds the flowery lea,
And a' is young and sweet like thee,
O, wilt thou share its joys wi' me,
And say thou'lt be my dearie, O?

2. The primrose bank, the wimpling burn,
The cuckoo on the milk-white thorn
The wanton lambs at early morn
Shall welcome thee, my dearie, O. ➜ ➜

64

Lassie Wi' The Lint-White Locks
advanced harp arrangement

Harp arrangement by Sylvia Woods

Words by Robert Burns

Moderately

3. And when the welcome simmer shower
Has cheer'd ilk drooping little flower
We'll to the breathing woodbine-bower
At sultry noon, my dearie, O.

4. When Cynthia lights, wi' silver ray
The weary shearer's hameward way;
Thro' yellow waving fields we'll stray,
And talk o' love, my dearie, O.

5. And when the howling wintry blast
Disturbs my lassie's midnight rest,
Enclasped to my faithfu' brest,
I'll comfort thee, my dearie, O.

The Lea-Rig
easy harp arrangement

Harp arrangement by Sylvia Woods

Words by Robert Burns

1. When o'er the hill the eastern star
Tells bughtin time is near, my jo,
And owsen frae the furrowed field
Return sae dowf and weary, O,
Down by the burn, where scented birks
Wi' dew are hanging clear, my jo,
I'll meet thee on the lea-rig
My ain kind dearie, O.

2. At midnight hour, in mirkest glen,
I'd rove, and ne'er be eerie, O,
If thro' that glen I gaed to thee,
My ain, my ain kind dearie, O!
Altho' the night were ne'er sae wild,
And I were ne'er sae weary, O,
I'd meet thee on the lea-rig,
My ain kind dearie, O. ➡ ➡

The Lea-Rig
advanced harp arrangement

Harp arrangement by Sylvia Woods

Words by Robert Burns

3. The hunter lo'es the morning sun
To rouse the mountain deer, my jo:
At noon the fisher takes the glen
Adown the burn to steer, my jo;
Gie me the hour o' gloamin grey -
It maks my heart sae cheery, O,
To meet thee on the lea-rig,
My ain kind dearie, O!

Leezie Lindsay
easy harp arrangement

Harp arrangement by Sylvia Woods

Some words by Robert Burns

Moderately

1. Will ye gang to the Hielands Leezie Lindsay?
Will ye gang to the Hielands wi' me?
Will ye gang to the Hielands, Leezie Lindsay,
My bride and my darling to be?

2. To gang to the Hielands wi' you, sir,
I dinna ken how that may be,
For I ken na' the land that ye live in,
Nor ken I the lad I'm gaun wi'. → →

Leezie Lindsay
advanced harp arrangement

Harp arrangement by Sylvia Woods

Some words by Robert Burns

Moderately

3. O Leezie, lass, ye maun ken little
If sae be that ye dinna ken me;
My name is Lord Ronald MacDonald,
A chieftain o' high degree.

4. She has kilted her coats o' green satin,
She has kilted them up to the knee;
And she's off wi' Lord Ronald MacDonald,
His bride and his darling to be.

Loch Lomond
easy harp arrangement

Harp arrangement by Sylvia Woods

Traditional

Slowly and sadly

1. By yon bonnie banks and by yon bonnie braes,
Where the sun shines bright on Loch Lomond;
Where me and my true love were ever wont to gae,
On the bonnie, bonnie banks of Loch Lomond.

CHORUS:
O, ye'll tak' the high road and I'll tak' the low road,
And I'll be in Scotland afore ye,
But me and my true love will never meet again,
On the bonnie, bonnie banks of Loch Lomond.

→ →

Loch Lomond
advanced harp arrangement

Harp arrangement by Sylvia Woods

Traditional

Slowly and sadly

2. 'Twas there where we parted in yon shady glen,
On the steep, steep side o' Ben Lomond,
Where in purple hue the Hieland hills we view,
And the moon comin' out in the gloamin'.

3. The wee birdies sing and the wild flowers spring,
And in sunshine the waters are sleepin';
But the broken heart it kens, nae second spring,
Tho' the waefu' may cease frae their greetin'.

Loch Tay Boat Song
easy harp arrangement

Harp arrangement by Sylvia Woods

Traditional

Slowly

72

1. When I've done my work of day and I row my boat away
Doon the waters o' Loch Tay as the evening light is fading
And I look upon Ben Lawers, where the after glory glows
And I think on two bright eyes and the melting mouth below.
She's my beauteous nighean ruadh, she's my joy and sorrow too
And although she is untrue, well I cannot live without her
For my heart's a boat in tow, and I'd give the world to know
Why she means to let me go, as I sing horee, horo.

(Lyrics continued on page 75) ➡ ➡

Loch Tay Boat Song
advanced harp arrangement

Harp arrangement by Sylvia Woods

Traditional

2. Nighean ruadh your lovely hair, has more glamour I declare,
Than all the tresses rare, 'tween Killin and Aberfeldy.
Be they lint white, brown or gold, be they blacker than the sloe,
They are worth no more to me, than the melting flake o' snow.
Her eyes are like the gleam, o' the sunlight on the stream
And the song the fairies sing, seems like songs she sings at milking.
But my heart is full of woe, for last night she bade me go,
And the tears begin to flow, as I sing horee, horo.

A Man's A Man For A' That
(Is There For Honest Poverty)
easy harp arrangement

Harp arrangement by Sylvia Woods

Words by Robert Burns

Moderately

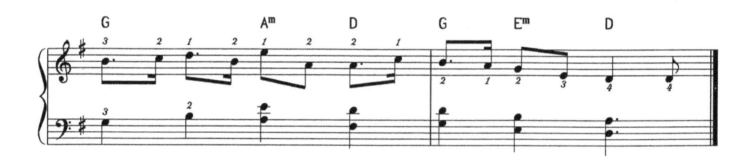

1. Is there for honest poverty
That hangs his head, an' a' that;
The coward slave, we pass him by,
We dare be poor for a' that!
For a' that, an' a' that,
Our toils obscure an' a' that,
The rank is but the guinea's stamp,
The man's the gowd for a' that.

2. What though on hamely fare we dine,
Wear hoddin grey, an' a' that?
Gie fools their silks, and knaves their wine,
A man's a man for a' that.

For a' that, an' a' that,
Their tinsel show an' a' that,
The honest man, tho' e'er sae poor,
Is king o' men for a' that.

3. Ye see yon birkie ca'd a lord,
Wha struts, an' stares, an' a' that;
Tho' hundreds worship at his word,
He's but a coof for a' that,
For a' that, an' a' that,
His ribband, star, an' a' that,
The man o' independent mind
He looks an' laughs at a' that. ➡ ➡

A Man's A Man For A' That
(Is There For Honest Poverty)
advanced harp arrangement

Harp arrangement by Sylvia Woods

Words by Robert Burns

Moderately

4. A prince can mak a belted knight,
A marquis, duke, an' a' that;
But an honest man's aboon his might,
Guid faith, he maunna fa' that!
For a' that, an a' that,
Their dignities an a' that,
The pith o' sense, an' pride o' worth,
Are higher rank than a' that.

5. Then let us pray that come it may,
As come it will, for a' that,
That sense and worth o'er a' the earth
Shall bear the gree an' a' that;
For a' that, an' a' that,
It's comin yet for a' that,
That man to man the world o'er
Shall brithers be for a' that.

My Heart's In The Highlands

easy harp arrangement

Harp arrangement by Sylvia Woods

Words by Robert Burns

1. My heart's in the Highlands, my heart is not here,
My heart's in the Highlands a-chasing the deer,
A-chasing the wild deer, and following the roe --
My heart's in the Highlands, wherever I go.

2. Farewell to the Highlands, farewell to the North --
The birthplace of valour, the country of worth:
Wherever I wander, wherever I rove,
The hills of the Highlands for ever I love.

3. Farewell to the mountains high cover'd with snow.
Farewell to the straths and green valleys below,
Farewell to the forests and wild-hanging woods,
Farewell to the torrents and loud-pouring floods!

My Heart's In The Highlands

advanced harp arrangement

Harp arrangement by Sylvia Woods

Words by Robert Burns

Portrait of Robert Burns by Alexander Nasmyth used by permission of the National Portrait Gallery, London

My Love Is Like A Red, Red Rose

easy harp arrangement

Harp arrangement by Sylvia Woods

Words by Robert Burns

Moderately, and tenderly

Lyrics are on page 109

My Love Is Like A Red, Red Rose
advanced harp arrangement

Harp arrangement by Sylvia Woods

Words by Robert Burns

Moderately, and tenderly

My Love She's But A Lassie Yet

easy harp arrangement

Harp arrangement by Sylvia Woods

Words by Robert Burns

Lightly

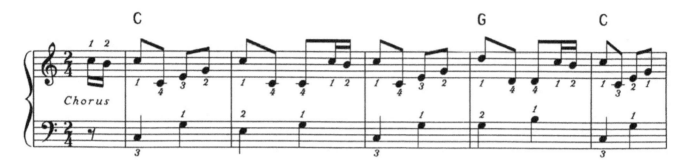

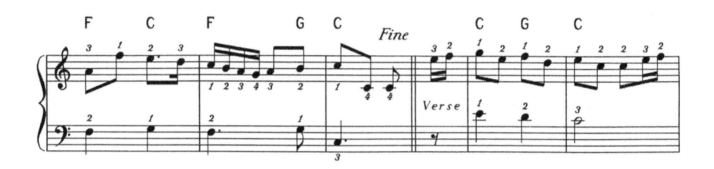

CHORUS:
My love, she's but a lassie yet,
My love, she's but a lassie yet!
We'll let her stand a year or twa,
She'll no be half sae saucy yet!

1. I rue the day I sought her, O,
I rue the day I sought her, O!
Wha gets her need na say he's woo'd,
But he may say he's bought her, O! ➔ ➔

My Love She's But A Lassie Yet

advanced harp arrangement

Harp arrangement by Sylvia Woods

Words by Robert Burns

Lightly

2. Come draw a drap o' the best o't yet,
Come draw a drap o' the best o't yet!
Gae seek for pleasure whare ye will,
But here I never missed it yet.

3. We're a' dry wi' drinkin' o't,
We're a' dry wi' drinkin' o't!
The minister kiss't the fiddler's wife --
He could na preach for thinkin' o't!

My Nanie, O
easy harp arrangement

Harp arrangement by Sylvia Woods
Slowly and tenderly

Words by Robert Burns

1. Behind yon hills where Stinchar flows
'Mang moors an' mosses many, O
The wintry sun the day has clos'd,
And I'll awa to Nanie, O.
The westlin wind blaws loud an' shill,
The night's baith mirk and rainy, O;
But I'll get my plaid, an' out I'll steal,
An' owre the hill to Nanie, O.

2. My Nanie's charming, sweet, an' young;
Nae artfu' wiles to win ye, O:
May ill befa' the flattering tongue
That wad beguile my Nanie, O!
Her face is fair, her heart is true;
As spotless as she's bonnie, O,
The op'ning gowan, wat wi' dew,
Nae purer is than Nanie, O. → →

My Nanie, O

advanced harp arrangement

Harp arrangement by Sylvia Woods

Words by Robert Burns

Slowly and tenderly

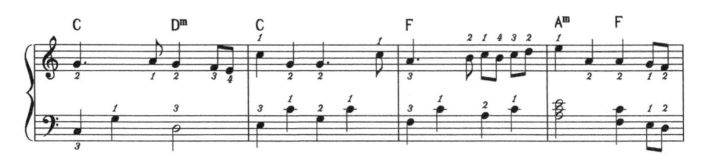

3. A country lad is my degree,
And few there be that ken me, O,
But what care I how few they be
I'm welcome aye to Nanie, O.
My riches a' 's my penny-fee,
An' I maun guide it cannie, O,
But warl's gear ne'er troubles me,
My thoughts are a' my Nanie, O.

4. Our auld guidman delights to view
His sheep and kye thrive bonnie, O,
But I'm as blythe that hauds his pleugh,
An' has nae care but Nanie, O.
Come weel, come woe, I care na by,
I'll tak' what Heav'n will sen' me, O,
Nae ither care in life have I,
But live, an' love my Nanie, O.

Rantin' Rovin' Robin   or   Dainty Davie

easy harp arrangement

Harp arrangement by Sylvia Woods

Robert Burns / Traditional

Moderately

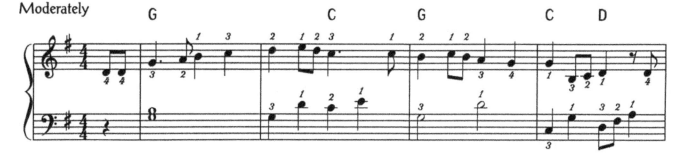

> Robert Burns' words for
> "Rantin' Rovin' Robin" are
> autobiographical.
> The traditional song "Dainty
> Davie" uses this same
> melody. You'll find those
> lyrics on the next page.

Rantin' Rovin' Robin

There was a lad was born in Kyle,
But whatna day o whatna style,
I doubt it's hardly worth the while
To be sae nice tae Robin.

CHORUS:
Robin was a rovin' boy,
Rantin', rovin', rantin', rovin'

Robin was a rovin' boy,
Rantin', rovin' Robin!

2. Our monarch's hindmost year
but ane
Was five-and-twenty days begun,
'Twas then a blast of Janwar wind
Blew hansel in on Robin.

3. "He'll hae misfortunes great an

sma'
But ay a heart aboon them a',
He'll be a credit tae us a':
We'll a' be proud o' Robin!"

4. "But sure as three times three
mak' nine,
I sware by ilka score and line,
This lad will surely love our kin',
So leeze me on thee, Robin!"

Rantin' Rovin' Robin   or   Dainty Davie

advanced harp arrangement

Harp arrangement by Sylvia Woods

Robert Burns / Traditional

Dainty Davie

1. It was in and through the window broads
And a' the tirlie-wirlies o't.
The sweetest kiss that e'er I got
Was from my dainty Davie.

CHORUS:
Oh, leeze me on your curly pow,
Dainty Davie, Dainty Davie
Leeze me on your curly pow,
My ain dear Dainty Davie.

2. It was doon amang my daddy's pease,
And underneath the cherry trees;

Oh, there he kist me as he pleased,
For he was my ain dear Davie.

3. When he was chased by a dragoon,
Into my bed he was laid doon,
I thocht him worthy o' his room,
For he's aye my dainty Davie.

Rattlin' Roarin' Willie

easy harp arrangement

Harp arrangement by Sylvia Woods

Words by Robert Burns

Lever harp players: set all the Fs as F naturals before you begin. Only the high F will change through the piece.
Pedal harp players: set all the pedals to natural before you begin.

Quickly and gaily

1. O rattlin', roarin' Willie,
   O, he held to the fair,
   An' for to sell his fiddle
   And buy some ither ware;
   But parting wi' his fiddle
   The saut tear blin't his e'e;
   And rattlin' roarin' Willie,
   Ye're welcome hame to me!

2. "O Willie, come sell your fiddle,
   O, sell your fiddle sae fine!
   O Willie, come sell your fiddle,
   And buy a pint o' wine!"
   "If I should sell my fiddle,
   The warld would think I was mad;
   For monie a rantin' day
   My fiddle and I hae had." ➔ ➔

Rattlin' Roarin' Willie

advanced harp arrangement

Harp arrangement by Sylvia Woods

Words by Robert Burns

Lever harp players: set all the Fs as F naturals before you begin. Only the high F will change through the piece.
Pedal harp players: set all the pedals to natural before you begin.

Quickly and gaily

3. As I cam by Crochallan,
I cannilie keekit ben;
Rattlin' roarin' Willie
Was sitting at yon boord-en';
Sitting at yon boord-en',
And amang guid company;
Rattlin', roarin' Willie,
Ye're welcome hame to me!

A Rosebud By My Early Walk
easy harp arrangement

Harp arrangement by Sylvia Woods

Words by Robert Burns

1. A rosebud by my early walk,
Adown a corn-inclosed bawk,
Sae gently bent its thorny stalk,
All on a dewy morning.
Ere twice the shades o' dawn are fled,
In a' its crimson glory spread,
And drooping rich the dewy head,
It scents the early morning.

2. Within the bush, her covert nest
A little linnet fondly prest,
The dew sat chilly on her breast,
Sae early in the morning.
She soon shall see her tender brood,
The pride, the pleasure o' the wood,
Amang the fresh green leaves bedew'd,
Awake the early morning. ➝ ➝

90

A Rosebud By My Early Walk

advanced harp arrangement

Harp arrangement by Sylvia Woods

Words by Robert Burns

3. So thou, dear bird, young Jeany fair!
On trembling string or vocal air
Shalt sweetly pay the tender care
That tents thy early morning!
So thou, sweet Rosebud, young and gay,
Shalt beauteous blaze upon the day,
And bless the parent's evening ray
That watch'd thy early morning.

The Rowan Tree
easy harp arrangement

Harp arrangement by Sylvia Woods

Words by Lady Nairne

Moderately

1. Oh rowan tree, oh rowan tree
Thou'lt aye be dear to me,
Entwined thou art wi' mony ties
O' home and infancy.
Thy leaves were aye the first of spring,
Thy flowers the simmers pride.
There was nae sic a bonnie tree
In a' the country side.
Oh rowan tree.

2. How fair wert thou in simmer time,
Wi' a' thy clusters white,
How rich and gay thy autumn dress,
Wi' berries red and bright!
On thy fair stem were mony names
Which now nae mair I see,
But they're engraven on my heart,
Forgot they ne'er can be.
Oh rowan tree. ➔ ➔

The Rowan Tree
advanced harp arrangement

Harp arrangement by Sylvia Woods

Words by Lady Nairne

Moderately

3. We sat aneath thy spreadin' shade,
The bairnies round thee ran,
They pu'd thy bonnie berries red,
And necklaces they strang;
My mither, oh! I see her still,
She smil'd our sports to see,
Wi' little Jeannie on her lap,
And Jamie at her knee.
Oh rowan tree.

4. Oh there arose my father's pray'r,
In holy ev'ning's calm,
How sweet was then my mother's voice,
In the "Martyrs" psalm!
Now a' are gane! we meet nae mair
Aneath the rowan tree,
But hallow'd thoughts around thee
Twine o' hame and infancy.
Oh rowan tree.

Scotland The Brave
easy harp arrangement

Harp arrangement by Sylvia Woods

Words by Cliff Hanley

In march tempo

Lyrics are on page 109

Scotland The Brave
advanced harp arrangement

Harp arrangement by Sylvia Woods

Words by Cliff Hanley

In march tempo

Scots Wha Hae
easy harp arrangement

Harp arrangement by Sylvia Woods

Words by Robert Burns

Resolutely. Either moderately, or with spirit

1. Scots wha hae wi' Wallace bled,
Scots wham Bruce has aften led,
Welcome to your gory bed,
Or to victorie!
Now's the day, and now's the hour;
See the front o' battle lour,
See approach proud Edward's pow'r --
Chains and slaverie!

2. Wha will be a traitor knave?
Wha can fill a coward's grave?
Wha sae base as be a slave?
Let him turn, and flee!

Wha for Scotland's King and Law
Freedom's sword will strongly draw,
Freeman stand or freeman fa',
Let him on wi' me!

3. By Oppression's woes and pains,
By your sons in servile chains,
We will drain our dearest veins
But they shall be free!
Lay the proud usurpers low!
Tyrants fall in every foe!
Liberty's in every blow!
Let us do, or dee!

Scots Wha Hae
advanced harp arrangement

Harp arrangement by Sylvia Woods

Words by Robert Burns

Resolutely. Either moderately, or with spirit

Robert the Bruce and Sir William Wallace

"Scots Wha Hae" has become the unofficial Scottish national anthem. Robert Burns wrote the words on August 1, 1793. It is said that he was inspired by his visit to the site of the Battle of Bannockburn. This 1314 battle was a celebrated victory for the Scottish troops, when Robert 1 (the Bruce) wiped out the English forces of King Edward II. Sir William Wallace (1272-1305), another Scottish hero mentioned in this song, was the subject of Mel Gibson's 1995 movie Braveheart.

Skye Boat Song

easy harp arrangement

Harp arrangement by Sylvia Woods
Moderately with accented rhythms

Words by Harold Boulton

Lyrics on page 109

Skye Boat Song
advanced harp arrangement

Harp arrangement by Sylvia Woods
Moderately with accented rhythms

Words by Harold Boulton

History on page 29

© 1997 by Sylvia Woods, Woods Music & Books, Inc.

99

Wae's Me For Prince Charlie
easy harp arrangement

Harp arrangement by Sylvia Woods

Words by William Glen

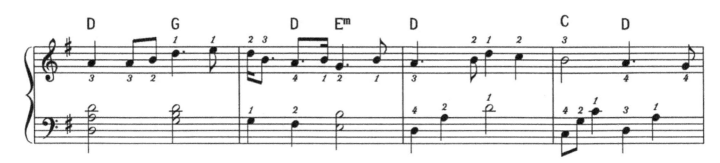

1. A wee bird cam' to our ha' door,
He warbled sweet and clearly,
An' aye the o'ercome o' his sang
Was "Wae's me for Prince Charlie!"
Oh! when I heard the bonnie, bonnie bird,
The tears cam' drappin rarely,
I took my bonnet aff my head,
For weel I lo'ed Prince Charlie!

2. Quoth I, "My bird, my bonnie, bonnie bird,
Is that a sang ye borrow:
Are those some words ye've learnt by heart,
Or a lilt o' dool an' sorrow?"
"Oh! no, no, no," the wee bird sang,
"I've flown sin' mornin' early;
But sic a day o' wind an' rain --
Oh! wae's me for Prince Charlie. → →

Wae's Me For Prince Charlie

advanced harp arrangement

Harp arrangement by Sylvia Woods

Words by William Glen

Moderately

3. "On hills that are by right his ain,
He roves a lanely stranger,
On every side he's press'd by want,
On every side is danger.
Yestreen I met him in a glen,
My heart maist burstit fairly,
For sadly changed indeed was he --
Oh! wae's me for Prince Charlie!

4. "Dark night cam' on, the tempest roar'd,
Loud o'er hills an' valleys,
An' where was't that your Prince lay down,
Wha's hame should been a palace?
He row'd him in a Highland plaid,
Which cover'd him but sparely,
An' slept beneath a bush o' broom -
Oh! wae's me for Prince Charlie!"

5. But now the bird saw some red coats,
An' he shook his wings wi' anger.
"Oh! this is no a land for me;
I'll tarry here nae langer!"
He hover'd on the wing a while
Ere he departed fairly,
But weel I mind the farewell strain
Was "Wae's me for Prince Charlie!"

The White Cockade
easy harp arrangement

Harp arrangement by Sylvia Woods

Words by Robert Burns

Like a march

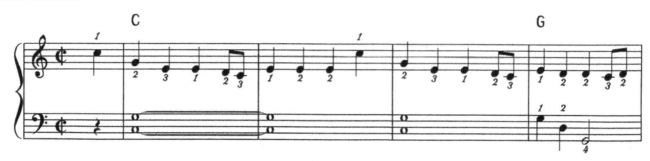

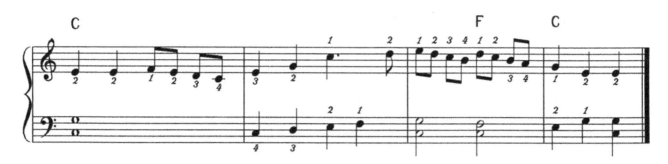

1. My love was born in Aberdeen,
The bonniest lad that e'er was seen;
But now he makes our hearts fu' sad --
He takes the field wi' his white cockade.

CHORUS:
O, he's a rantin', rovin' lad!
He is a brisk an' a bonnie lad!
Betide what may, I will be wed,
An' follow the boy wi' the white cockade!
➛ ➛

The White Cockade
advanced harp arrangement

Harp arrangement by Sylvia Woods

Words by Robert Burns

Like a march

2. I'll sell my rock, my reel, my tow,
My guid gray mare and hawkit cow,
To buy mysel a tartan plaid,
To follow the boy wi' the white cockade!

Will Ye No Come Back Again?
easy harp arrangement

Harp arrangement by Sylvia Woods

Words by Lady Nairne

Slowly, with expression

1. Bonnie Charlie's noo awa';
Safely owre the friendly main
Mony a heart will break in twa,
Should he ne'er come back again?

CHORUS:
Will ye no come back again?
Will ye no come back again?
Better lo'ed ye canna be,
Will ye no come back again?   ➜ ➜

Will Ye No Come Back Again?

advanced harp arrangement

Harp arrangement by Sylvia Woods

Words by Lady Nairne

Slowly, with expression

2. Ye trusted in your Hieland men,
They trusted you, dear Charlie!
They kent your hiding in the glen,
Death and exile braving.

3. English bribes were a' in vain
Tho' puir and puirer we maun be;
Siller canna buy the heart
That aye beats warm for thine and thee.

4. We watch'd thee in the gloamin' hour,
We watch'd thee in the mornin' grey;
Tho' thirty thousand pounds they gie,
Oh, there is nane that wad betray!

5. Sweet's the laverock's note, and lang,
Liltin' wildly up the glen;
But aye to me he sings ae sang --
"Will ye no come back again?"

Ye Banks And Braes

easy harp arrangement

Harp arrangement by Sylvia Woods

Words by Robert Burns

Lyrics are on page 109

Ye Banks And Braes
advanced harp arrangement

Harp arrangement by Sylvia Woods

Words by Robert Burns

The Birks Of Aberfeldy (pages 12-13)
5. Let Fortune's gifts at random flee,
They ne'er shall draw a wish frae me;
Supremely blest wi' love and thee
In the birks of Aberfeldy.

Bonnie Dundee (pages 20-21)
3. There are hills beyond Pentland, and lands beyond
Forth,
Be there lords in the south, there are chiefs in the
north:
There are brave Duinnewassals, three thousand times
three,
Will cry: "Hey, for the bonnets o' Bonnie Dundee."

4. Then awa' to the hills, to the lea, to the rocks,
Ere I own a usurper I'll crouch with the fox;
And tremble, false Whigs, in the midst o' your glee,
Ye hae no seen the last o' my bonnets and me.

Bonnie Wee Thing (pages 22-23)
CHORUS: Bonnie wee thing, cannie wee thing,
Lovely wee thing, wert thou mine.
I wad wear thee in my bosom,
Lest my jewel it should tine!

1. Wishfully I look and languish
In that bonnie face o' thine;
And my heart it stounds wi' anguish,
Lest my wee thing be na mine.

2. Wit and Grace and Love and Beauty,
In ae constellation shine;
To adore thee is my duty,
Goddess o' this soul o' mine!

Corn Rigs Are Bonnie (pages 32-33)
1. It was upon a Lammas night,
When corn rigs are bonnie, O,
Beneath the moon's unclouded light,
I held awa' to Annie, O.
The time flew by, wi' tentless heed,
Till 'tween the late and early, o;
Wi' sma' persuasion she agreed
To see me thro' the barley, O.

CHORUS: Corn rigs, an' barley rigs,
Corn rigs are bonnie, O,
I'll ne'er forget that happy night,
Amang the rigs wi' Annie, O.

2. The sky was blue, the wind was still,
The moon was shining clearly, O,
I set her down, wi' right good will,
Amang the rigs o' barley, O:
I kent her heart was a' my ain:
I lov'd her most sincerely, O;
I kiss'd her owre and owre again,
Amang the rigs o' barley, O.

3. I lock'd her in my fond embrace;
Her heart was beating rarely, O;
My blessings on that happy place.
Amang the rigs o' barley, O!
But by the moon and stars so bright.
That shone that hour so clearly, O!
She ay shall bless that happy night.
Amang the rigs o' barley, O.

4. I hae been blythe wi' comrades dear;
I hae been merry drinking, O;
I hae been joyfu' gath'rin' gear;
I hae been happy thinkin', O:
But a' the pleasures e'er I saw,
Tho' three times doubl'd fairly, O;
That happy night was worth them a',
Amang the rigs o' barley, O.

John Anderson, My Jo (pages 56-57)
7. John Anderson, my jo, John, frae year to year we've
past,
And soon that year maun come, John, will bring us to
our last;
But let not that affright us, John, our hearts were ne'er
our foe,
While in innocent delight we liv'd, John Anderson,
my jo.

8. John Anderson, my jo, John, we clamb the hill
thegither;
And mony a canty day, John, we've had wi' ane
anither;
Now we maun totter down, John, but hand in hand
we'll go,
And sleep thegither at the foot, John Anderson, my jo.

The Keel Row (pages 58-59)
3. He wears a blue bonnet, blue bonnet, blue bonnet,
He wears a blue bonnet, a dimple's in his chin.
And Weel may the keel row, the keel row, the keel
row.
Weel may the keel row, that my lad's in.

My Love Is Like a Red, Red Rose
(pages 80-81)
1. My love is like a red, red rose,
That's newly sprung in June.
O my love is like a melodie,
That's sweetly play'd in tune.
As fair art thou, my bonnie lass,
So deep in love am I,
And I will love thee still, my dear,
Till a' the seas gang dry.
Till a' the seas gang dry, my love,
Till a' the seas gang dry,
And I will love thee still, my dear,
Till a' the seas gang dry.

2. Till a' the seas gang dry, my dear,
And the rocks melt wi' the sun!
And I will love thee still, my dear,
While the sands o' life shall run.
And fare thee weel, my only love,
And fare thee weel a while!
And I will come again my love,
Tho' 'twere ten thousand mile!
Tho' 'twere ten thousand mile, my love!
Tho' 'twere ten thousand mile!
And I will come again my love,
Tho' 'twere ten thousand mile!

Scotland The Brave   (pages 94-95)
1. Hark, when the night is falling;
Hear! hear the pipes are calling
Loudly and proudly calling,
Down thro' the glen.
There where the hills are sleeping,
Now feel the blood a-leaping,
High, as the spirits of the
Old Highland men.

CHORUS: Towering in gallant fame,
Scotland my mountain hame,
High may your proud standards Gloriously wave.
Land of my high endeavor, Land of the shining silver,
Land of my heart forever, Scotland the brave.

2. High in the misty Highlands,
Out by the purple islands,
Brave are the hearts that beat
Beneath Scottish Skies.
Wild are the winds to meet you,

Staunch are the friends that greet you,
Kind as the love that shines
From fair maidens' eyes.

Skye Boat Song   (pages 98-99)
CHORUS: Speed bonnie boat, like a bird on the wing,
Onward the sailors cry!
Carry the lad that's born to be king,
Over the sea to Skye!

1. Loud the winds howl, loud the waves roar,
Thunder claps rend the air,
Baffled our foes stand by the shore,
Follow they will not dare.

2. Though the waves leap, soft shall ye sleep,
Ocean's a royal bed;
Rocked in the deep, Flora will keep
Watch by your weary head.

3. Many's the lad fought on that day,
Well the claymore could wield
When the night came, silently lay
Dead on Culloden's field.

4. Burned are our homes, exile and death
Scatter the loyal men;
Yet, e'er the sword cool in the sheath,
Charlie will come again.

Ye Banks And Braes   (pages 106-107)
1. Ye banks and braes o' bonnie Doon,
How can ye bloom sae fresh and fair?
How can ye chant, ye little birds,
And I sae weary fu' o' care!
Thou'll break my heart, thou warbling bird,
That wantons thro' the flow'ring thorn!
Thou minds me o' departed joys,
Departed never to return.

2. Aft hae I rov'd by bonnie Doon
To see the rose and woodbine twine,
And ilka bird sang o' its love,
And fondly sae did I o' mine.
Wi' lightsome heart I pu'd a rose,
Fu' sweet upon its thorny tree!
And my fause lover staw my rose --
But ah! he left the thorn wi' me.

GLOSSARY

a' - all
abeigh - at bay
aboon - above
acquent - acquainted
adown - down
ae - one
a-faulding - gathering the sheep
aff - off
aft, aften - often
aiken - oak; oaken
ain - own
aince - once
amang - among
ane - one, an
anither - another
artless - innocent, without guile
a's - all is
asklent - aside
auld - old
auld lang syne - days of long ago
awa' - away
ay, aye - always
bairnies, bairns - children
baith - both
bandsters - a party of harvesters
bawk - strip left unploughed
be - pay for ("Auld Lang Syne")
bear the gree - take first place,
        be victorious
ben - parlour, into a parlour
birkie - boastful fellow
birk; birks, birken - birch tree(s)
blaws - blows
bleer - blear, bedim
blear'd - bleary
blin'; blin't - blind, blinded
blink; blinks - shine; shines
bluid; bluidy - blood; bloody
blythe - carefree, gay
bogle - spectre, hide and seek
bonnie, bonny - pretty, handsome
boord-en' - table end
braes - hillsides, slopes
braid - broad
braw, brawly - handsome, brave;
brawest - most handsome
brent - smooth
brithers - brothers

broads - see "window broads"
broom besoms - brooms made of
        broom twigs
bughtin - folding (gathering the
        sheep in the fold)
bughts - sheepfold
burn, burnie - small stream, brook
ca', ca'd - call, called
ca' the yowes - drive the ewes
caddie - messenger boy
cam - came
canna - cannot
cannie - gentle, skillfully
cannilie - cautiously
canny - skillful
canty - cheerful
cauld - cold
clamb - climb
claymore - large two-edged sword
clead; cleeds - clothe, clothes
cockade - ribbon worn on the hat
coft - bought
coof - fool
coost - did cast
cot - cottage
craig - crag
creel - basket
crouse - brisk, bold
Cynthia - moon
daffin' - fun
dee - die
den - ravine
dine - dinner-time
dingle - small, deep wooded valley
dinna - don't
dool - tragedy, alas
doon - down
douce - kind, dear, sober
dowf - dull
dowie - sorrowful
drap, drappie - drop
Duinnewassals - gentlemen
e'e - eye
een - eyes, evening
e'en - even, evening, might as well
eerie - forlorn, frightened
fa'; fa's - fall or tread; falls
fain - glad, joyous
faithfu' - faithful
fause - false
fiere - chum, companion

fleech - flatter
flooers - flowers
frae - from
fu' - full
gabbin' - chatting
gae, gang; gaun - go; going
gaed; gane, - went; gone
gar; gart - make, cause; made
gath'rin gear - money-making
gear - possessions
Geordie - King George
ghaist - ghost
gie; gie's - give; give us
gin - if, whether
glen; glens - valley; valleys
gloamin' - twilight
gowan; gowans - daisy; daisies
gowd - gold, money
grat - wept
gree - see "bear the gree"
greetin' - crying, weeping
gude, guid - good
guidman - husband, master of a
        household
ha', ha's - hall, halls, houses
hae, ha'e - have
hairst - harvest
hairt - heart
haith - faith
hame - home
hamely - homely
han' - hand
hansel - a gift to bring good luck
        to something new
hauds - holds
hawkit - white-faced cow
heugh - crag
Hielands - Highlands
hies - hurries
hing - hang
hirplin - limping, hobbling
hizzie - young woman
hoddin grey - coarse home-made
        woolen cloth
ilk; ilka - each; every
ither; ithers - other; others
Janwar - January
jo - joy, darling
keekit - peeked, looked
keel - flat-bottomed ship
ken(s); kent - know(s); knew

kin' - kind
kirk - church
knowes - knolls
kye - cattle
lade - load
laird - landowner
Lammas - harvest festival
      celebrated on August 1
Land o' the Leal - Heaven
lanely - lonely
lang(s); langer- long(s); longer
lave - the rest, the others
laverock - lark
lea - meadow
lea-rig - meadow ridge
leal - true, faithful, pure
      (see "Land o' the Leal")
lear - knowledge
leeze - blessing on, commend me
leglin - milk pail
leish - active, athletic
lightsome - merry
linn; linns - waterfall; waterfalls
lint-white - flaxen
loanin' (green loanin') - commons
lo'e; lo'ed; lo'es - love; loved; loves
loot - let
lour -threatening
lowpin - leaping
lyart - grizzled, old
mair - more
maist - most, almost
mak; maks - make; makes
'mang - among
maun - must
maunna fa' - cannot claim
mavis - thrush, lark
meikle - much
mettled - spirited
minds - reminds
mirk; mirkest - dark; darkest
mither - mother
monie, mony - many
muckle - much
murlain - fisherman's basket
na; nae; nane - not; no, none;
      none
nighean - darling
nocht - nothing
noo - now
nought - nothing

o'er-come - refrain
o't - of it
oor - our
oot - out
owre - over
owsen - oxen
paidl'd - waded, paddled
palfrey - a gentle saddle horse
parritch - porridge
peerie - very small
penny-fee - wages
philabeg - Highland kilt, plaid
pint-stowp - pint-size tankard
pith - force, strength
plack - four pennies Scots
pleugh - plow
pou'd, pu'd - pulled
pow - head
puir; puirer - poor, poorer
rantin - lively, noisy
ribband - ribbon, badge
rig, rigs - ridge, ridges
rinnin' - running
rins - runs
rowan - ash
row'd - rolled, wrapped
rowes - runs, flows
ruadh - red-haired
runkled - wrinkled
sabbing - sobbing
sae - so, if
saft - soft
sair - sore
saut - salt
scorning - feigned scolding
shaws - woods
shearer's - reaper's
shill - shrill
sic - such
siller - silver
simmer - summer
sin - since
skeigh - disdainful
sloe - blackthorn
sma' - small
smoor'd - smothered
snaw - snow
staw - stole
stounds - throbs, aches
stowlins - secretly
stown - stolen

strang - strong
straths - wide river valleys
swankies - strapping young men
syne - since, then, ago
tae - to
tak' - take
tapsalteerie - topsy-turvy
tent - watch over, heed, tend
tentless - careless
thegither - together
thocht - thought
tine, tint - lose, lost
tirlie-wirlies - whirlygigs
tocher - dowry
toun - town
tow - flax, rope
trew, trews - tartan trousers
trig - trim, neat
twa - two
unco - very
wa' - wall
wad - would
waefu' - sorrow, wailing
wae's - woe is
wan - won
ware - things
wark - work
warld; warldly - world; worldly
wa's - walls
wauk - am sleepless
wauken - awaken
waukin - always awake, sleepless
waur - worse
wede - carried off (to their death)
weel - well
weets - wets
westlin - western
wha; wham; wha's - who; whom;
      whose
whare, whaur - where
wi' - with
willie-waught - friendly drink
wimpling - meandering
window broads - shutters
woodbine - honeysuckle
wrang - wrong
yestreen - yesterday evening
yon - that
yowes - ewes

Index of First Lines

Other Books By Sylvia Woods